# Embracing
# Forgiveness

## Other Women of Faith Bible Studies

*Celebrating Friendship*
*Discovering Your Spiritual Gifts*
*Experiencing God's Presence*
*Finding Joy*
*Growing in Prayer*
*Knowing God's Will*
*Strengthening Your Faith*

WOMEN OF FAITH™
BIBLE STUDY SERIES

# Embracing
# Forgiveness

Written by

# TRACI MULLINS

ZondervanPublishingHouse

*Grand Rapids, Michigan*

*A Division of* HarperCollins*Publishers*

*Embracing Forgiveness*
Copyright © 1998 by Women of Faith, Inc.

Requests for information should be addressed to:

📖 ZondervanPublishingHouse
*Grand Rapids, Michigan 49530*

ISBN: 0-310-21341-X

*General Editor, Traci Mullins*
*Cover and interior illustration by Jim Dryden*
*Interior design by Sue Vandenberg Koppenol*

*Printed in the United States of America*

01 02 03 04 /❖ EP/ 10 9 8 7 6 5

# CONTENTS

# FOREWORD

The best advice I ever received was in 1955. I was twenty-three. Somebody had the good sense to say to me, "Luci, if you want to give yourself a gift, learn all you can about the Bible. Start going to a Bible class and don't stop until you have some knowledge under your belt. You won't be sorry." Having just graduated from college, I was living with my parents, and together we drove more than twenty miles to attend that class. We went four nights a week for two years. I've *never* been sorry.

Nothing I've ever done or learned has meant more to me than those classes. Unless I was on my deathbed, I didn't miss. I went faithfully, took notes, absorbed everything like a sponge, asked questions relentlessly, and loved *every* minute! (I probably drove the teacher crazy.)

Today, more than forty years later, this wonderful storehouse of truth is my standard for living, giving, loving, and learning. It is my Rock and Fortress, the pattern for enjoying abundant life on earth, and for all eternity. I know what I believe, and why. I'm open to change on my tastes, personal opinions, even some of my choices. But change my biblical convictions? No way! They're solid and secure, based on God's inerrant, enduring, and unchanging Word. There's nothing like learning God's truth. As he says, it sets you free.

Women of Faith Bible studies are designed to help you deal with everyday problems and issues concerning you. Experienced and wise women who, like the rest of us, want to know God intimately, have written these lessons. They encourage us to dig into the Scriptures, read them carefully, and respond to thought-provoking questions. We're invited to memorize certain verses as sources of support and guidance, to hide his Word in our heads and hearts.

The clever ideas in these studies make me smile. The stories move my spirit. There are valuable suggestions in dealing with others, quotations that cause me to stop and think. The purpose of every activity is to put "some knowledge under your belt" about the Bible and its relevance for life *this very day.*

Give yourself a gift. Grab your Bible, a pencil, notepad, cup of coffee . . . maybe even a friend . . . and get started. I assure you—you'll *never* be sorry.

LUCI SWINDOLL

# HOW TO USE THIS GUIDE

Women of Faith Bible studies are designed to take you on a journey toward a more intimate relationship with Christ by bringing you together with your sisters in the faith. We all want to continue to grow in our Christian lives, to please God, to be a vital part of our families, churches, and communities. But too many of us have tried to grow alone. We haven't found enough places where we feel safe to share our heartaches and joys and hopes. We haven't known how to support and be supported by other women in ways that really make a difference. Perhaps we haven't had the tools.

The guide you are about to use will give you the tools you need to explore a fundamental aspect of your walk with God *with* other women who want to grow, too. You'll not only delve into Scripture and consider its relevance to your everyday life, but you'll also get to know other women's questions, struggles, and victories—many similar, some quite different from your own. This guide will give you permission to be yourself, to share honestly, to care for one another's wounds, and laugh together when you take yourselves too seriously.

Each of the six lessons in this guide is divided into six sections. Most you'll discuss as a group; others you'll cover on your own during the week between meetings.

*A Moment for Quiet Reflection.* The questions in this section are meant to be answered in a few minutes of privacy sometime before you join your group each week. You may already carve out a regular time of personal reflection in your days, so you've experienced the refreshment and insight these times bring to your soul. However, if words like "quiet," "reflection," and "refreshment" have become unfamiliar to you, let this guide get you started with the invaluable practice of setting aside personal time to think, to rest, to pray. Sometimes the answers you write down to the questions in this section will be discussed as a group when you come together; other times they'll just give you something to ponder deep within. Don't neglect this important reflection time each week, and include enough time to read the introduction to the lesson so you'll be familiar with its focus.

*Knowing God's Heart.* The questions in this section will take you into the Bible, where you and the women in your group can discover God's heart and mind on the subject at hand. You'll do the Bible study together, reading the Scriptures aloud and sharing your understanding of the passage so all of you can learn together what God has to say about your own heart and life, right now. While you don't need to complete the study questions prior to each group session, it will be helpful for you to read through this part of the lesson beforehand so you can begin thinking about your answers. There is a lot to cover in each lesson, so being somewhat familiar with the content before your meetings will save your group time when you actually do your study together.

*Friendship Boosters.* A big part of why you've come together is to deepen your friendships with other women and to support each other in meaningful ways. The questions and activities in this section are designed to link you together in bonds of friendship, faith, and joy. Whether you are meeting the other women in your group for the first time or are old friends, this section will boost the quality and pleasure in your relationships as well as give you opportunities to support each other in practical ways.

*Just for Fun.* God's plan for our lives certainly isn't all work and no play! Central to being a woman of faith is cultivating a joyful spirit, a balanced perspective, and an ability to enjoy life because of God's faithfulness and sovereignty. Every week you'll be given an idea or activity that will encourage you to enjoy your journey, laugh, and lighten your load as you travel the path toward wholehearted devotion together.

*Praying Together.* Nothing is more important than asking God to help you and your friends as you learn how to live out his truths in your lives. Each time you get together you'll want to spend some time talking to him about your individual and mutual concerns.

*Making It Real in Your Own Life.* You'll respond to these questions or activities on your own after group meetings, but don't consider them just an afterthought. This section is critical because it will help you discover more ways to apply what you've learned and discussed to your own life in the days and weeks ahead. This section will be a key to making God's liberating truths more real to you personally.

In each section, space is provided after each question for you to record your answers, as well as thoughts stimulated by others' answers during group discussion. While you can gain wisdom from completing parts of this guide on your own, you'll miss out on a lot of the power—and the fun!—of making it a group experience.

One woman should be designated as the group facilitator, but she needn't have any training in leading a Bible study or discussion group. The facilitator will just make sure the discussion stays on track, and there are specific notes to help her in the "Leader's Guide" section at the back of this book. Keeping your group size to between four and eight participants is ideal because then it will be possible for everyone to share each week. The length of time you'll need to complete the lessons together will depend largely on how much the participants talk, so the group facilitator will need to monitor the time to keep it under ninety minutes. The facilitator can also speed up or slow down the group time by choosing to skip some discussion questions or concentrate longer on others. If you decide to do this study in a larger group or Sunday school class, split up into smaller groups for discussion. Especially make sure no one gets left out of the process of building friendships and having fun!

Now that you've studied the map, your journey should go smoothly. Celebrate being women of faith as you travel together. *Enjoy!*

*Get rid of all bitterness, rage and anger, brawling and slander, along with every form of malice. Be kind and compassionate to one another, forgiving each other, just as in Christ God forgave you. Be imitators of God, therefore, as dearly loved children and live a life of love, just as Christ loved us and gave himself up for us as a fragrant offering and sacrifice to God.*
EPHESIANS 4:31–5:2

# INTRODUCTION
## Tall Orders

You've just plopped down in your usual spot in the fourth pew, and you're basking in the few moments of peace before the worship service begins. Nothing big on your mind, no demons rattling your cage. And then you see her sweep into the third pew on your far right. Your stomach clenches and the bile rises in your throat. Amazing how you can almost forget what she did and go about the business of living, only to trip headlong into angst the moment you see her from across a room.

Just as you're beginning to replay her wrongs against you (how many times has it been now?), the words of the Lord you've come to worship leap unbidden into your mind: "You have heard that it was said to the people long ago, 'Do not murder, and anyone who murders will be subject to judgment.' But I tell you that anyone who is angry with his brother will be subject to judgment" (Matt. 5:21–22).

*Uh-oh.* The knot in your stomach just cinched tighter.

Another night punctuated by nightmares. Will it never end? How many times do you have to see his face hovering above you, monsterishly contorted by the shadows? It's been thirty years since he last molested you. Why can't you forget?

As you curl into a fetal position under the covers, you plot for the zillionth time to get back at him. There's got to be a way to make him pay. Maybe when he and Mom are over for dinner this weekend you can get in some extra-sharp barbs that will leave him bleeding. They won't begin to balance the scales, but at least you can remind him he's not off your hook. . . .

Suddenly your midnight musings are rudely interrupted by the Bible's words: "Do not repay anyone evil for evil. . . . 'If your enemy is hungry, feed him; if he is thirsty, give him something to drink'" (Romans 12:17, 20).

*Say what? But he . . . Hey, just a minute here. . . .*

In this world brimming with sinners, none of us escapes being on the receiving end of harm. And because we are sinners ourselves, we hurt others as well. The harm may come in the form of a garden-variety cross word from someone we love, diabolical manipulation from an enemy intent on destroying us, or our own hardness of heart—but Jesus promises that it will indeed come (John 16:33). On top of that distressing news, he adds a number of exacting statements like, "If you forgive men when they sin against you, your heavenly Father will also forgive you. But if you do not forgive men their sins, your Father will not forgive your sins" (Matt. 6:14–15).

Now isn't that just a bit much? I mean, some people are such rodents. Does God really expect us to put up with them? Be kind to them? Forgive them? *Love them?* Even if we'd like to, we're not saints. Aren't Jesus' high commands a little out of our league?

And then there's the issue of our own sin. If the folks who like us only knew some of the things we've done, how much we've hurt some of the people we should have loved a whole lot better. Can we ever make up for our mistakes? Will those we've harmed even let us try? And what about God? Does he *really* see us as far removed from our transgressions as one end of the earth is from the other (Ps. 103:12)?

Few teachings in Scripture are more difficult to understand and practice than the ones about forgiveness. Lewis Smedes, author of a popular classic *Forgive and Forget*, writes, "The act of forgiving, by itself, is a wonderfully simple act; but it always happens inside a storm of complex emotions. It is the hardest trick in the whole bag of personal relationships."

If Smedes knows this, then surely Jesus did, too, when he commanded us to practice this art form diligently. Maybe he really does comprehend what we're up against when our wounds are stinging and our hearts are bleeding. Maybe he can give us some real help when we're ostracized by those we've hurt or swamped by self-recrimination.

If you've ever balked at the Bible's tall orders concerning "turning the other cheek" when people offend you, loving those who've hurt you most, or embracing a grace that seems too good to be true, then this study is for you. It won't answer all your questions or give you clear-cut advice on how to handle every difficult relationship or internal hang-up. The Bible's teachings on forgiveness are so rich that they could never be digested in one sitting—or in one book. But we can learn a lot just by opening our hearts and minds and swallowing even small morsels of what the Word has to offer. The God of the universe is the ultimate expert on the subject of forgiveness; it's what his Son's whole life on earth was about. No one could be more clear on the fact that forgiving carries an exorbitant price tag— and buys the finest gifts worth having.

Want to know what they are? Come along on the steep but rewarding journey ahead—the way to forgiveness.

# Forgive and Forget?

W e've all heard the horror stories about hurting people who've been given advice by well-meaning but gravely misguided believers.

- "I understand that he hit you last night, but God says you are to turn the other cheek and submit to your husband."
- "Yes, you were abused, but that was twenty years ago. Get over it! Besides, he *is* your father, and the Bible says we're supposed to honor our parents."
- "Forgiveness is simply a decision made in obedience to Jesus' command. Just do it. If her offense still bothers you after that, then you must not have been sincere."
- "If you've really forgiven her, then you'll forget what she did and carry on the relationship as before. It doesn't matter whether or not she's sorry; the Bible says you are to love her and forgive her seventy times seven!"

Perhaps you've gotten some similar direction yourself—or you've given it in your earnest desire to offer biblical counsel. As believers we want to imitate God, as Scripture commands (Eph. 5:1). We know we are to love one another as he has loved us, so sometimes we harness ourselves to the heaviest yoke within reach and trudge forward in our valiant attempt to obey his toughest commandments.

But is that what he expects? Then what did he mean when he told us to come to him for rest because his yoke is easy and his burden is light

(Matt. 11:28–30)? Perhaps we make his commands to love and forgive more rigorous than he meant them to be. Perhaps in our sincere desire to please him, we've perverted part of his intent.

In this lesson we'll explore what biblical forgiveness is and what it is not. You may find that you've been pulling a load you need to leave on God's shoulders.

*Love is the power behind forgiveness. But it does not work the way a lot of people suppose. Love is not a soft and fuzzy sentiment that lets people get away with almost everything, no matter what they do to us. Love forgives, but only because love is powerful.*

LEWIS B. SMEDES

# A Moment
# for Quiet Reflection

**1.** Make room for at least fifteen minutes of private time and settle in to ask yourself some questions. What do you think forgiveness is? How does it look? Reflect on your personal definitions and write them down.

**2.** In what specific ways has your perspective on what it means to forgive been influenced by what your family or religion has taught you?

**3.** Do you see these influences as positive or negative or both? Why?

# Knowing God's Heart

**1.** As a group, discuss what you feel and believe about the following common conceptions of forgiveness. Do you agree with them or not? Why?

- Forgiveness means forgetting about the offense.

- Forgiveness involves excusing the offender.

- Forgiveness requires giving up the desire for vengeance.

- Forgiveness is about freeing oneself from the past.

- Forgiveness means "letting bygones be bygones."

- Forgiveness requires accepting the offender just as he is.

- Forgiveness results in reconciliation of a broken relationship.

**2.** Are any of the definitions from Question 1 on the list you made in "A Moment for Quiet Reflection"? Share with the group some of your personal conceptions that are the same or different.

3. Besides Jesus himself, few people in Scripture teach us more about forgiveness than Joseph does. One of two sons born to Jacob and Rachel, Joseph was the envy of his brothers, the other eleven sons of Jacob. Joseph was Jacob's favorite, and a bit spoiled and full of himself, so out of jealousy and spite his brothers sold him to some merchants they met along a road. "He's been killed by wild beasts," they lied to their father—(*and good riddance*, they thought). Little did they know that their little brother was sold again, this time to an Egyptian official named Potiphar.

God's favor was on Joseph, a handsome and intelligent seventeen-year-old, and in no time he was put in charge of everything Potiphar owned. After Potiphar's wife double-crossed Joseph, he spent over a decade in prison. But through a series of divine events the young Hebrew slave got the favorable attention of Pharaoh and eventually became the ruler of all of Egypt.

Enter Joseph's brothers stage left. Hoping to avoid starvation during the famine at home, the ten oldest trekked to Egypt to buy food from the guy in charge. Joseph recognized them instantly, but they didn't know him. After testing their character through a few tricky schemes, Joseph revealed his identity.

Read Genesis 45:1–15 aloud together. When Joseph came clean, how did his brothers respond? Why?

**4.** Compare Joseph's actions in verses 3 and 4. What is significant about the way he relates to his brothers in verse 4?

**5.** Joseph feels and expresses a great deal of emotion right before he reveals his identity. What does this intensity suggest about the consequences of withholding forgiveness and the probable results of finally extending it?

**6.** In verse 4 we are given one more key insight into the nature of forgiveness. What do the last five words of this verse imply?

**7.** In spite of the fact that Joseph had suffered and had spent a good part of his life in captivity because of his brothers' actions, he looked at his entire experience in a positive light. What do verses 5–8 suggest about how he did this? (Also take a moment to read Genesis 50:19–21, which reaffirms Joseph's perspective.)

**8.** Because of his perspective on his suffering, Joseph was able to let his cruel brothers "off the hook." What do you think is the specific lesson here about the nature of forgiveness?

**9.** Joseph not only reassured his brothers of his goodwill, but he invited them to bring all their relatives and flocks to live in Egypt at his expense so they would not starve during the famine. Before sending them back to Canaan to fetch his father, Jacob, and all their stuff, Joseph demonstrated his complete forgiveness once more by embracing and kissing the men who had once shown no regard whatsoever for his life. What do verses 14 and 15 suggest about how a fully reconciled relationship might look and feel?

**10.** It is critical to understand that the reconciliation between the victim and perpetrators in this story did not come as easily as these few verses might suggest. Before Joseph revealed his identity and welcomed his brothers back into his life, he put them through the paces to discern just who he was dealing with. Had the boys who sold him off for a few pieces of silver become men whose hearts were just as dark? Or had his brothers changed? Would they be capable of engaging in a "safe" relationship with him in the future? During your own Bible reading time in the week ahead, you might want to read the entire account in Genesis 42–44 of how Joseph tested his brothers. For now, what do you think Genesis 44:33–34 indicates about the heart of at least one of his brothers?

**11.** Of all the people who have harmed you, consider who is hardest for you to forgive. What, specifically, has made it so hard? Try to answer the question, "If I forgive, then . . ."

**12.** Help each other evaluate the statements you just made in light of what you've learned in this lesson about the nature of forgiveness. Can you see ways in which you've misunderstood what God requires of you? Discuss any ways in which what you've learned helps you move a step closer to forgiving the person who harmed you.

> *When we forgive it is not just for the sake of others.*
> *Often it is also for our sake.*
>
> ROB PARSONS

# Friendship Boosters

**1.** Take a few moments to exchange phone numbers, addresses, and e-mail addresses (if you have them).

**2.** On a small slip of paper, write down a statement that expresses a belief you've held about forgiveness that you now see may need to be altered in light of biblical truth. Pair up with the woman on your right and exchange papers. After you've read each other's statements, share how your beliefs have been similar to or different from your partner's. If you have time, briefly swap stories about how the belief you wrote down has caused you confusion, trouble, or heartache in a relationship.

# Just for Fun

While studying a subject as serious and sometimes painful as forgiveness, you'll want to help each other keep perspective. No matter what each of you is dealing with in terms of a broken relationship, painful memories, or unresolved guilt, life is also full of beauty, love, and reasons to celebrate. In the week ahead, buy a funny greeting card for the woman you shared with during "Friendship Boosters" and mail it to her. Be part of a "laugh network" with the women in your group so you can keep each other from becoming emotionally bogged down as you continue to explore the important subject at hand.

# Praying Together

Come back together as a group and pray that God will give each of you the willingness and courage to embrace what he has to teach you about forgiveness in the weeks ahead. Include a specific prayer for the woman whose paper you're holding: "Lord, help Kathy let go of the assumption that she'll be abused again if she forgives her offender." "God, show Judy that you have a loving plan for her life even though she has been harmed." Affirm together that the love of God is greater than the pain of this world.

> *Laughter is like changing a baby's diaper—*
> *it doesn't permanently solve any problems, but it*
> *makes things more acceptable for a while.*
> BARBARA JOHNSON

# Making It Real
## in Your Own Life

**1.** Now that you've gained some insight from the Word and from other women about the nature of forgiveness, review what you wrote in "A Moment for Quiet Reflection." If you are ready to revise any of your beliefs, do so by crossing out words or writing in new ones to clarify your position.

**2.** Since we have only just begun our study, you probably have nagging questions about forgiveness in general or about how it relates to a specific person in your life. Write down at least three questions and offer them up to God in faith that he will give you helpful insight in the weeks ahead.

---

*If any of you lacks wisdom, he should ask God,*
*who gives generously to all without finding fault,*
*and it will be given to him.*

JAMES 1:5

---

# Hey, That's Not Fair!

Most of us know the story of the prodigal son, the young upstart who demanded his inheritance before his father was even in the ground and then ran off to squander the nest egg on whatever pleasures suited his fancy. Broke and hungry and caked with mud, he trudges home to grovel, knowing he's broken his father's heart but hoping the man will at least allow him to be a servant and earn his keep. How surprised he must have been when his father not only forgave his foolishness and selfishness but also threw him a big party as he welcomed him back into the family circle with full rights and privileges!

Who doesn't love a happy ending? So we usually stop there when we think about the lost son's story. But there is something else going on as the party goes into full swing. "Meanwhile, the older son was in the field" (Luke 15:25). And he wasn't celebrating his bratty little brother's homecoming.

Who among us hasn't identified with the older brother at one time or another? The prophet Jeremiah certainly could relate when he questioned God about the scales of justice: "You are always righteous, O LORD, when I bring a case before you. Yet I would speak with you about your justice: Why does the way of the wicked prosper? Why do all the faithless live at ease?" (Jer. 12:1). The age-old question of why "bad" people so often thrive while "good" people suffer is one that sticks in the craw when we're commanded to give up our ill will toward those we resent. Why should we?! Where is the justice? Where is the price tag that should be firmly affixed to our enemy's offense?

The God of all justice understands such questions. Let's see what he has to say in response.

> *Let God handle those you would like to manhandle in your hate. If they need teaching, let God teach them. If they need rescuing from their own stupidity, let God rescue them. If they need saving from their own crazy wickedness, let God save them. What you need is healing from the infection of malice left over from the open wounds they left in your life.*
>
> LEWIS B. SMEDES

# A Moment
# for Quiet Reflection

**1.** Is there anyone whose behavior has negatively affected
you who hasn't seemed to "pay a price" for his or her trans-
gression? If so, put on your lawyer's hat and write a "brief"
to God about it. Review the facts and suggest how you
think justice might be better served.

**2.** What were your emotions as you wrote?

# Knowing God's Heart

**1.** Read Luke 15:25–32 together. According to verse 28, what was the older son's initial response to the news that a lavish party was being thrown in his little brother's honor? Pretend you are viewing the scene in this verse as an objective observer and discuss how the characters might have acted and felt.

**2.** Review the older son's tirade against his father one statement at a time. What do the following comments in verse 29 seem to indicate about this man's relationship with his dad:

- "All these years I've been slaving for you and never disobeyed your orders."

- "You never gave me even a young goat so I could celebrate with my friends."

**3.** What further insight into this son's heart do you gain from his final comment in verse 30?

**4.** What three things did the father try to communicate to his son in verses 31–32?

**5.** Some interpreters say that the characters in this parable symbolize God, a repentant sinner, and a Pharisee. In this light, what do we learn about the character of God from the father in this story? (You may want to review the entire account in Luke 15:11–32.)

**6.** What do we learn from the younger son about the kind of attitude we're to have when approaching God for forgiveness?

7. What does the older brother's experience suggest we avoid and/or strive for in our relationship with God and others?

8. If you feel comfortable, briefly share with the group your "case" against the person you wrote about in "A Moment for Quiet Reflection."

9. Now imagine that God the Father is standing before you, preparing to speak to you about your feelings and behavior in response to the person you resent, just as the father in this story addressed his son. What do you think he would say to you?

**10.** Have one woman read aloud 1 John 1:8–10 and another read 1 John 2:9–11. What further insight do the apostle's words give you into what was amiss in the older brother's response?

**11.** In what ways do you see yourself in the older brother? (Don't feel self-conscious—we all resemble him at times!)

**12.** If you still consider yourself more virtuous than the people who have hurt you (and you may be!), the apostle Paul has some words of encouragement for you. Have someone read 1 Corinthians 4:4–5 aloud. What promise can you hold on to even in the midst of what appears to be gross injustice?

> *It is the hope of glory which makes suffering bearable.*
> JOHN R. W. STOTT

# Friendship Boosters

Most women who have experienced the benefits of close friendship with other women agree on at least one thing: trustworthy women friends are "safe harbors" in whose presence understanding and support can be found. Pair up with the woman directly across from you and risk sharing with each other a specific challenge you're facing in a relationship with someone who has done you harm. If you're not dealing with a particular hurt or difficult relationship right now, talk about one from the past and how you handled it—your way or Jesus' way.

# Just for Fun

The prodigal's brother suffered from a personal blind spot and a lack of spiritual insight. Get ready to go on a "blind woman's walk." Decide which one of you will wear a blindfold, and have that person pick out an object in another room that she'll guide her partner to while in the dark. Make sure her blindfold is on tight, then follow her as she makes her way to her destination—hesitantly and inefficiently, no doubt. Don't give her any clues about direction, but do make sure she doesn't hurt herself! Once you both "arrive" (if you ever do!), remove the blindfold and rejoin the group. Discuss what this exercise teaches regarding the importance of having clean spiritual lenses when we view ourselves, other people, and the road of life. How does having the wrong lenses affect our ability to direct others toward Christ?

# Praying Together

Come back together as a group and turn out the lights so the room is as dark as possible. Then spend some time together humbly asking God to remove any spiritual blindness that is causing you to hold on to judgments or resentments that are hurting you and your relationships. When you are finished praying, keep your eyes closed while the leader turns the lights back on. Close your prayer time with short statements of gratitude for the light of God that illuminates the path ahead.

*Amazing grace, how sweet the sound*
*That saved a wretch like me!*
*I once was lost but now am found,*
*Was blind but now I see!*

JOHN NEWTON

# Making It Real in Your Own Life

1. If there is someone you are jealous of or you feel is blessed by God even though he or she doesn't "deserve" it, write that person's name down on a small piece of paper and put it in your pocket or in a prominent place today. Every time you see that name or think about that person, ask God to lavish on him or her everything you want for yourself or the person you love the most. Yes, this is HARD—it may even make you sick to your stomach at first! But if you're willing to try it, you might be amazed at the power prayer and goodwill have to transform your malice into genuine benevolence.

**2.** Sometimes we become so obsessed with what's "fair" that we can overfocus on even the smallest of infractions. Life is not fair, and some battles aren't meant to be fought. In light of the following words from Dr. Richard Carlson, consider whether some of the resentments you're carrying around are related to "small stuff" that isn't worth fighting over.

> Certainly there will be times when you will want or need to argue, confront, or even fight for something you believe in. Many people, however, argue, confront, and fight over practically anything, turning their lives into a series of battles over relatively "small stuff." There is so much frustration in living this type of life that you lose track of what is truly relevant. The tiniest disagreement or glitch in your plans can be made into a big deal if your goal (conscious or unconscious) is to have everything work out in your favor.

*Once we begin to see how often we subtly dismiss others because they don't live up to our standards, we can slowly start to let go of our judgments and get back to trying to figure out what we came here to do. And then get on with it.*
ELAINE ST. JAMES

# An Eye for an Eye!

Once upon a time there was a lady who had had it. She was sick and tired of feeling like the brunt of her boss's ill will. He didn't like her; she knew it. Not that she'd done anything specific to raise his ire. She just seemed to rub him the wrong way. He was uncommunicative; she liked to talk. He was meticulous; she was a bit, well, "imprecise." He had a temper; she was a peacemaker. And she was a believer; he was not. Spending the majority of her time with him every day was bad enough, but yesterday was the last straw.

The day had started out uneventfully: he'd come in to the building in one of his "moods," passed her desk with a grunt that sounded something like "good morning," and shut himself up in his office. She knew he was under pressure to finish a project, but today was the deadline for his signature on some contracts she'd put on his desk last week. Later in the day when she poked her head in to get his attention she could feel the tension in the room, but nothing could have prepared her for the hostile response she got.

He attacked. His face turned scarlet and contorted with rage as he slammed his full coffee cup down on his desk, sending papers flying and coffee splattering over important documents. Later she could hardly remember what he'd said; none of it made much sense. But she couldn't forget the sense of persecution she felt. What a jerk! She was only trying to do her job.

She recalled some Old Testament laws that made a lot of sense about now: "If anyone injures his neighbor, whatever he has done must be done to him: fracture for fracture, eye for eye, tooth for tooth. As he has injured the other, so he is to be injured" (Lev. 24:19–20). Ooh, that sounded good. Made sense. Sounded more than fair. In fact, it felt good just to roll the words around in her mind. She could picture herself on her steed, riding into combat with a holy battle cry on her lips: "An eye for an eye, a tooth for a tooth!" Those Hebrews might have been a bit too physical with their violence, but the war whoop made her feel powerful!

Who hasn't been tempted to withhold forgiveness in order to punish? After all, "they deserve it," and being the avenger feels a lot less vulnerable than being the victim.

But then our friend remembered something Jesus said: "If someone strikes you on the right cheek, turn to him the other also" (Matt. 5:39). *Yikes.* Now what? As a Christian, what in the world did God want her to do this morning as she headed off to work with a foolish, angry man?

As we'll see, there is no one simple answer. But Jesus did give us some unusual guidelines that can help us renew our strength when we've had it and live out forgiveness in tangible ways. Let's explore what that "turning the other cheek" stuff is all about.

---

*By not forgiving, I chain myself to a desire to get even, thereby losing my freedom. A forgiven person forgives. This lifelong struggle lies at the heart of the Christian life.*
HENRI NOUWEN

# A Moment
# for Quiet Reflection

**1.** Have you ever had an experience similar to our fed-up friend's? A time when you felt unduly harassed or wounded? We've all been hurt at one time or another, and we've all felt the desire to get even. Write a late-breaking news story about one of your experiences. Give it a headline and answer the journalist's who-what-when-where questions in your account of the events. Choose the perspective you prefer: objective reporter or tabloid tattler.

**2.** Give some thought to what penalty you think might be appropriate for your offender. If you could concoct the perfect punishment to fit his or her crime, what would it be? (Don't feel too guilty if you relish this exercise just a little!)

# Knowing God's Heart

**1.** One at a time, share your news story headlines with the group. Ask at least one volunteer to read her account in grisly detail, considering how you would feel toward her offender if you were in her shoes.

**2.** Now read Matthew 5:38–47 together. Jesus often quoted Hebrew Scripture when he was teaching, sometimes to reaffirm the truths it expressed, other times to reveal how the new covenant differed from the old. In Old Testament days, God's people were expected to follow to the letter the laws handed down through Moses. The Pentateuch (the first five books in the Bible) contains a slew of explicit regulations that were designed to set apart the people who followed them as a unique nation, holy unto God. The "eye for an eye" thing was one of God's edicts—and there were lots more that gave the Jews insight into the perfect justice of God's character. (How about the one in Exodus 21:29 that demanded death by stoning for the guy who let his unruly bull roam and gore some innocent bystander? A little harsh maybe, but hey, he shouldn't have been so irresponsible.)

When Jesus refers to the ancient scale-balancing command in Matthew 5:38, he is preparing to introduce a whole new way for God's people to differentiate themselves from the world around them. How do you suppose his listeners responded to his radical teaching?

**3.** Jesus' instruction about how to handle abuse and injustice is still radical today. Discuss what thoughts and emotions came up for you when you read this passage. Does it seem like good advice? Why or why not?

**4.** Jesus usually used parables and word pictures when he taught great truths; he drew from what was familiar in contemporary culture to drive home his points to whomever was listening. Considering that Jesus probably was not advising his disciples to literally let some bully smack them up both sides of the head, what do you think he meant when he told them to turn the other cheek when someone hurt them?

**5.** Verses 39–42 describe a basic attitude we're to possess and express as followers of Jesus. How would you describe this attitude in a sentence or two? Make note of what you come up with as a group.

6. It's easy, isn't it, to feel affection for and be nice to the people who like us and treat us well. As Jesus points out, that attitude and response comes naturally even to a godless heathen. What do you think is Jesus' intent when he ends this particular series of thoughts with the intimidating words, "Be perfect, therefore, as your heavenly Father is perfect"?

7. The apostle Paul has another piece of advice for us in his letter to the Romans. Have someone read Romans 12:17–19 aloud. What additional counsel might you give our distraught employee in light of these verses?

8. One reason we naturally rush to avenge ourselves or those we love when damage is done is that we fear the perpetrator will "get away with it." That injustice is unacceptable, so we devise strategies to make him pay. (We may not carry out our plans, but we readily give God advice about what he should do on our behalf!) According to Romans 12:19, why is it so important for us to resist inventing our own schemes to effect justice?

**9.** Some of the hardest interpersonal conflicts to deal with are those between believers. When we are hurt by a brother or sister in the faith, the pain can be especially intense because we are members of the same spiritual family, and we expect better from each other. But because imperfect people inevitably cause each other harm, Jesus spelled out how we are to deal with a fellow believer when he or she sins against us. Have someone read Matthew 18:15–17 out loud. What three specific instructions are given to the "plaintiff" when harm has been done?

**10.** If the "respondent" refuses to acknowledge his crimes and be restored to his brother, what are you to do? Why?

**11.** Because we all have a bent toward vengeance when we're hurt, sometimes it's easier to follow Jesus' instruction in Matthew 18:17 than it is to obey his command in Luke 17:3–4. Do you think these verses are ordering us to put up with abuse? Why or why not?

**12.** Review the story at the beginning of this lesson and spend some time brainstorming about what advice you would give the woman who works for a jerk. How might she follow Jesus' and Paul's instructions as she continues to relate to her boss in the months ahead? (Keep in mind that Christlike love is, in essence, bold and creative. There is no one "right" answer for what our friend should do, so think of several ways she might express her Christianity in this difficult relationship.)

**13.** God does not expect us to "grin and bear it" or "keep a stiff upper lip" when we are hurt. Discuss how the following quote from Barbara Johnson relates to the process of forgiveness: "Sometimes allowing yourself to cry is the scariest thing you'll ever do. And the bravest. It takes a lot of courage to face the facts, stare loss in the face, bare your heart, and let it bleed."

*Forgiving is love's revolution against life's unfairness. When we forgive, we ignore the normal laws that strap us to the natural law of getting even and, by the alchemy of love, we release ourselves from our own painful pasts.*
LEWIS B. SMEDES

# Friendship Boosters

Midway through this guide we've swallowed some big truths and reflected on realities and relationships that may have unearthed some old hurts or exacerbated some fresh wounds. Check in with at least one other woman in your group this week by phone or e-mail and ask her how she's doing on her way to forgiveness. Ask her what she needs: a word of encouragement, an hour's getaway from her own thoughts, something to laugh about, someone to celebrate her progress with. Give to her from your heart.

# Just for Fun

Without a full comprehension of all the cultural, social, and spiritual implications of living as a follower of Christ during New Testament days, it's hard to relate to the high price many of Jesus' friends paid for being "different." Dare to be different in a fun way that will probably only cost you some puzzled, disgusted, or incredulous stares from passersby. Schedule a time between now and the next session to dress and groom yourself in a way that's sure to get some gawks. As a group or in twos or threes, go out to a public place like a mall or restaurant and just "be" your socially unacceptable selves for a while. Notice the responses you get.

> *This is life, not a funeral service. Have some fun with it. Enter into it. Participate. Experiment. Take a risk. Be spontaneous. Do not always be so concerned about doing it right, doing the appropriate thing. Do not be so fearful and proper.*
> MELODY BEATTIE

# Praying Together

Pray for each other in regard to living out your Christian faith in a world that can sometimes be hostile and hurtful. Ask God to fill your hearts with wisdom, grace, benevolence, and forgiveness. Close your prayer time by saying Reinhold Niebuhr's famous prayer aloud together:

> God, grant me the serenity to accept the things I cannot change; courage to change the things I can; and the wisdom to know the difference. Living one day at a time; accepting hardship as a pathway to peace; taking, as Jesus did, this sinful world as it is, not as I would have it; trusting that you will make all things right if I surrender to your will; that I may be reasonably happy in this life and supremely happy with you forever in the next. Amen.

---

*Love is essentially a movement of grace to embrace those who have sinned against us. It is the offer of restoration to those who have done harm, for the purpose of destroying evil and enhancing life. Love can be defined as the free gift that voluntarily cancels the debt in order to free the debtor to become what he might be if he experiences the joy of restoration.*

DAN B. ALLENDER

# Making It Real
# in Your Own Life

**1.** Review the delicious discipline you came up with in "A Moment for Quiet Reflection" in light of what you've learned in this lesson. Are you still certain it's the ideal punishment for the person who hurt you? Why or why not?

**2.** Consider some of the advice or insight you got from your friends at the end of your last Bible study session. What one or two ideas did you take away to practice when you are dealing with someone who pushes your buttons or smacks a tender part of your soul? Remember, the other person's response is not the issue here; your unique expression of God's love is.

**3.** If you were going to die tomorrow and could leave behind a message to the person who's hurt you the most in this life, what would it be? Why?

# Fire Up the Barbecue

The apostle Paul doesn't try to sugarcoat the horror and mess that evil creates in our world every day. He doesn't ask us to ignore it, minimize it, excuse it, or tolerate it. Rather, he urges us to *hate* it (Rom. 12:9). But in our passionate disgust we are also to "cling to what is good." If evil is so horrific, then it makes no sense for those of us who are ringing in the kingdom to add insult to injury. That's why retaliating against those who've hurt us is off-limits.

Our desire for justice is not incompatible with Christian love, however; God, the supreme lover, has every intention of sweeping the universe free of evil when he crushes Satan under our feet (Rom. 16:20). He doesn't excuse evil, but warns, "But unless you repent, you too will all perish" (Luke 13:3). Sin is *bad;* it deserves to be punished, and it will be. It's just that it's *his* prerogative to mete out justice in his own perfect way. It's not our business. Besides, as sinners ourselves we're bound to throw aside mercy in our quest for justice. Left to our own devices, we are apt to crush hidden good along with obvious evil and condemn sinners God is committed to saving (2 Peter 3:9).

Okay—so far, so good. Maybe we can trust God to take care of the big issues of crime and punishment and resist the urge to be as nasty to our offenders as they were to us. Perhaps we can do our part to live in peace with other sinners and even choke out some prayers for those we'd rather curse. We might even dip deep enough into our redeemed hearts to draw up the divine love that longs to see our most cruel enemy touched and transformed by the power of God's grace.

But Paul wasn't done when he told us to revoke revenge and be the "good guys." He goes on to something a whole lot harder when he insists that we are actually to *do good things* for those who've hurt us. Christian love is not just merciful; it is actively, passionately involved in a wicked world.

Take a deep breath and come along on the next leg of the way to forgiveness. It may be the steepest, but it can be the most rewarding.

*People who've been looked at by Christ are never free again to live the way their poor, tired hearts sometimes wish they could. He loves us too much to ask less of us than he does, and in ten thousand ways he pursues us with "a love that will not let us go."*

JIM MCGUIGGAN

# A Moment for Quiet Reflection

**1.** At this point in our study of biblical forgiveness, some of the questions nagging you in the "Making It Real in Your Own Life" section of Lesson 1 may have been answered. Referring to the questions you wrote down a few weeks back, what helpful insights have you gained in relation to them?

**2.** If questions remain, or new ones have surfaced, write them down and ask God to give you clarity in the days ahead. The answers to some questions will only be fully understood in heaven, but God has promised to give us wisdom in our daily lives (James 1:5).

# Knowing God's Heart

**1.** Read Paul's second piece of advice on how to deal with evil in Romans 12:20–21. What do you think is the significance of the instruction to give our enemies food and drink when they are hungry or thirsty?

**2.** If you were to show kindness and generosity to someone who has hurt you deeply, what do you think his or her internal response would be? What might yours be if the roles were reversed?

**3.** At first glance it may appear that Paul is giving us the advice our mothers or grandmothers may have dished out at one time or another: "Just be nice, dear. Put on a happy face." But biblical commands are never shallow or pointless. There's a method to the "madness" Paul is suggesting. Doing good in the face of evil may feel crazy and dangerous in the moment, but there is a divine purpose at work. What's your guess about what it is?

**4.** In answer to that question, Paul gives us a curious word picture, drawn from the wisdom of the wisest man in history, King Solomon. Now, firing up the barbecue and getting the coals red hot so you can dump them on top of the person who's done you wrong doesn't sound very nice. Do you think Paul is recommending hurting your enemy? Why or why not?

**5.** Theologians give various interpretations for the metaphor of "burning coals," but the consensus seems to be that in the context of doing good to an enemy, the coals symbolize his burning shame in response to kindness from the one he has harmed. (Peter reiterates this concept in 1 Peter 3:15–16). Of course, the most evil of sinners may refuse to feel shame or admit their wrongs, but by "doing good" we give the wicked an invitation and opportunity to repent and change for the better. As a group, discuss how Christ's death on the cross was the ultimate example of this "heaping burning coals" concept.

**6.** In *The Message*, Eugene Peterson translates the intriguing directive this way: "If you see your enemy hungry, go buy him lunch; if he's thirsty, bring him a drink. *Your generosity will surprise him with goodness*" (Prov. 25:21–22, emphasis added). How is the element of surprise a key to someone's repentance? How was it involved in your own salvation?

**7.** Dr. Dan Allender defines forgiveness as "the free gift that voluntarily cancels the debt in order to free the debtor to become what he might be if he experiences the joy of restoration." Discuss ways you are "becoming what you might be" because of Christ's bold act of forgiveness. What might you have become if he had not canceled your debt?

**8.** Romans 12:21 summarizes the biblical teaching on the purpose of loving our enemies. Have someone read the verse aloud once again. Why is Paul recommending an active rather than passive stance toward those who do harm?

**9.** Discuss how you think this instruction fits together with the concept of "turning the other cheek." Consider Jesus' example as he lived and died on earth.

**10.** Have someone read the challenging words of David Atkinson aloud: "Forgiveness is a dynamic concept of change. It refuses to be trapped into a fatalistic determinism. It acknowledges the reality of evil, wrong, and injustice, but it seeks to respond to wrong in a way that is creative of new possibilities. Forgiveness signals an approach to wrong in terms, not of peace at any price, nor of a destructive intention to destroy the wrongdoer, but of a willingness to seek to reshape the future in the light of the wrong, in the most creative way possible." In light of everything you've learned about biblical forgiveness so far, discuss why it is, of necessity, dynamic, creative, and overflowing with hope.

> *Love is an act of forgiveness in which evil is converted*
> *to good and destruction into creation.*
> HENRI NOUWEN

# Friendship Boosters

**1.** It's pretty hard to be objective and creative when it comes to incinerating the sin in our enemy's heart by killing him with kindness, so we can all use a little help from our friends. Divide into groups of two or three (different combinations than last week) and spend some time on creative problem solving. Help each other come up with some specific acts of kindness that might fry the hair off your enemies' heads while inviting them to open the door to divine transformation. Make note of the ideas you could use with a particular person who's hurt you.

**2.** Read Psalm 19:9–11 together. Encourage each other by sharing ways in which you have experienced—or hope to experience—the value, sweetness, and reward of following biblical direction in the realm of loving your enemies.

# Just for Fun

It's time to take a break from all the heavy stuff we've been thinking about for the past several weeks. Whew! If we have accepted God's amazing grace and embraced the forgiveness of the Christ who willingly died in order to invite us to eternal life, then we have reason to celebrate no matter how much frustration and pain this imperfect world serves up. Marilyn Meberg reminds us that the development of a laugh attitude begins internally. It is built on the unshakable foundation of God's incomparable love for us.

As an affirmation of your faith in this perfect love and permanent security, take Marilyn's "divine prescription" for a crushed spirit. Have a volunteer begin a giggle session with the smallest "heh-heh." Chime in with your own giggles and guffaws, even if you have to fake it. Keep it up for a minute or so and watch the group dissolve into hysterics.

# Praying Together

Spend some time thanking God for his surprising, amazing grace. One at a time, offer one-sentence prayers of gratitude such as "God, thank you for never giving up on your enemies—including me." "Lord, I praise you for your infinite creativity in the way you deal with each of us." End your prayer time with "Amen," followed by the loudest "Hallelujah!" you can shout out in unison. (If your first one's a little feeble, try again!)

> *The sound of laughter is God's hand upon a troubled world.*
> BARBARA JOHNSON

# Making It Real in Your Own Life

**1.** Choose one "burning coal" from the ones you and your friends came up with in "Friendship Boosters" and plan a way to use it with someone who has never repented of the pain he or she caused you. If possible, carry out your plan this week. Remind yourself that your kindness is not intended to "sweep things under the rug" of denial, but to incinerate the part of your enemy's heart that is keeping him or her from experiencing the love that transforms evil into good.

    If you're not ready to take this step because of fear or anger that is still simmering in your heart, will you consider asking God to help you become willing as he continues to strengthen you in your faith?

**2.** Sometimes we can't interact with our enemies in cunning, redemptive ways because they are inaccessible through illness, distance, or death. If this is your situation, think of a symbolic or invisible way you can do good to your enemy. Write a letter you don't send, pray for him or her every day for a month, paint a picture that represents your forgiveness. Be creative!

> *To hang onto a resentment is to harbor a thief in the heart. By the minute and by the hour, resentment steals the joy we could treasure now and remember forever. It pilfers our energy to celebrate life—to face others as messengers of grace rather than ambassadors of doom. We victimize ourselves when we withhold forgiveness.*
> ERNIE LARSEN AND CAROL LARSEN HEGARTY

# Drop the Rock

*I*f God hates evil, then how can he love sinners? If even our best, most devoted, sinful human friend gets fed up with us at times, then how can the perfect God of the universe embrace us, warts and all? When we begin to comprehend even an inkling of the holiness of God, then our only response to his gracious love can be startled, stunned, stupefied wonder. And, ultimately, jubilation!

Have you ever given someone a gift they didn't use or enjoy? Either they didn't appreciate what it cost you in terms of cash or caring, or they were so self-conscious in their "oh, you shouldn't haves" that they never clasped the gift to their heart in humble joy. Either way, you both lost out on the delight of love shared, grace extended.

Considering what an exorbitant price God paid to be able to dwell intimately with us on our lowly plane, he must grieve over the combination of our shame and pride that sometimes keeps him at arm's length. When he sees us trudging up the steepest hills of life with a forty-pound rock of guilt and remorse strapped to our back, he must shake his head. Why do we foolishly, stubbornly refuse to dump off our rocks at his holy quarry where he pulverizes every pebble and boulder of sin into dust that dissipates on the wind of his grace?

Yes, our Father in heaven is perfect, holy, utterly beyond the reach of the grimy hands of humanity. But "while we were *still sinners*, Christ died for us" (Rom. 5:8, emphasis added). God's beloved Son stripped off his glory and hurtled through the heavens to pour out his hallowed blood like a river whose current sweeps us back to our Source. Because of Jesus, we are welcome to accept the Father's invitation to come home. Because of Jesus, we can drop the rock. Because of Jesus, we must. The only appropriate response of sinners saved by grace is to lay down our burdens, straighten our backs, and jump for joy!

*If you want God's fire to burn brightly in your heart,*
*take out yesterday's ashes.*

BARBARA JOHNSON

# A Moment
# for Quiet Reflection

**1.** Make a soothing, hot cup of something to hold on to and curl up in your favorite chair. Close your eyes and invite the "guilt monsters" that lurk in the back of your mind to come forward into the light. Name them one by one.

**2.** Now write down the names of these pesky residents. Some of them might be downright menacing, always threatening to crush out the embers of the joy of your salvation. Whoever they are, it's time to call them out of hiding and learn how to banish them from the dark corners of your soul.

# Knowing God's Heart

**1.** As a forgiven sinner, bought at the price of Christ's blood, how free do you feel of guilt and condemnation? Rate yourself on a scale of one to ten (one for heavily oppressed, ten for joyfully liberated), and share your score with the group.

| 1 | 2 | 3 | 4 | 5 | 6 | 7 | 8 | 9 | 10 |
|---|---|---|---|---|---|---|---|---|----|

**2.** Review your "guilt inventory" from "A Moment for Quiet Reflection" and discuss the character of the joy-stealers that have taken up residence in your soul. Are they irksome insects that buzz in your consciousness? Carping crones that keep you beaten down with their incessant accusations? Bellowing bullies that pin you up against the wall with threats of violence? Just what kind of internal enemies are you up against?

3. Now read John 8:1–11 together. The woman John tells us about here clearly had a lot to contend with from outside herself. The most religious guys in town had just dragged her in front of the most sought-after rabbi around and asked him if they could go ahead and take her out with the sharpest rocks they could find. What do you suppose was going on *inside* this woman as she was brought before Jesus?

4. We aren't told what Jesus was writing in the dust at his feet, but what might we infer about what he was thinking and feeling as the religious guys quizzed him about issues of law and justice from his general comportment?

5. Our Savior had an uncanny ability to surprise and silence the self-righteous folks of his time. Why do you suppose his response to the religious teachers and Pharisees in verse 7 left them dumb and deflated?

**6.** After the men had dispersed with their tails between their legs, Jesus addressed the lone woman for the first time. He could have filled her ear with a whole lot of explanation and instruction, but instead he asked her two simple questions. Why do you think he did this?

**7.** The rest of their exchange is brief and to the point. Discuss what the woman's few words might suggest about her.

**8.** What do Jesus' two final declarations imply about how he saw the whole situation?

**9.** We can only guess at what happened to the woman after Jesus sent her on her way. What do you think her life was like in the aftermath of their encounter? Give reasons for your opinions.

**10.** Think about a time in your life when you stood before Jesus, wrapped in a cloak of sin and shame. How did you feel? What did you do? What was the result of your encounter with grace? Ask for a few volunteers to share their experience.

**11.** Discuss the following quote from the Talmud, the authoritative book of Jewish tradition: "A sense of shame is a lovely thing in a man. Whoever has a sense of shame will not sin so quickly; but whoever shows no sense of shame in his face, his father surely never stood on Mount Sinai." In what ways can guilt and shame serve us well?

**12.** Have someone read Leviticus 26:11–13 (NIV) aloud. What does God want the results of grace to be in our lives?

> *To live tied to the past is to live in a prison; it is to live*
> *carrying a weight on one's back; it is to sit like a bird in*
> *a cage gazing at blue skies through an open door.*
>
> ROB PARSONS

# Friendship Boosters

**1.** Pair up with the woman whose birthday is closest to yours and tell her about one of your "internal enemies"—only as much detail as you're comfortable with. As you compare the size and shape of these particular "rocks" you've each been hauling around, talk about why you haven't laid them down once and for all. What specifically is keeping you from stopping off at God's quarry?

**2.** Whatever your reasons for keeping the weight of your sin and guilt strapped to your back, realize that you are not unique. Everyone has had trouble "dropping the rock" at times. Share a personal experience or a bit of advice with your friend that might help her loosen her grip on her heavy hunk. As you extend grace to each other, you might just find it flowing back toward you.

# Just for Fun

Schedule a time in the week ahead to put on your rock-hound clothes and go on a group hunt for craggy treasures. Choose a destination where you'll find a variety of stones, and start collecting. Designate a central spot where you can deposit your stash, and be sure to ask another woman for help if you find a particularly heavy specimen you want to add to the pile. After twenty minutes have passed, meet at your "quarry" and enjoy a healing ritual together. One at a time, pick up a rock that suits your fancy and hold it tight (or hug it tight if it's one of those boulders!). Spend a few moments in silence, reflecting on what you've learned or been reminded of in this lesson about the forgiveness of God. Then, with one voice, say "Because of Jesus!" with confidence and joy. Drop your rocks.

Now party! Go out for ice cream to celebrate the sweetness of God's love.

# Praying Together

God's grace is lavish, and his forgiveness makes our stained hearts white as snow. He sent his Son as a priceless gift to win our hearts, and he welcomes us home with great rejoicing. *However*, we aren't invited to barge into his hallowed halls and put our grimy fingerprints all over the walls. Our hands must be clean before we enter, and the only water that can do the job is the Living Water. God's forgiveness is not "free"; it was bought at an outrageous price—the shed blood of God himself. And the only way to enjoy the liberation it gives is to humbly acknowledge the precious gift and grasp it to our hearts with unspeakable gratitude.

No matter what your crimes, no matter how dirty you feel, there is a shower of grace waiting for you if you are willing to step under the sparkling stream. A broken and contrite heart is all you need bring with you.

King David staked his hope on the character of God when he threw himself on God's mercy after committing adultery with Bathsheba. As a group, encourage each other to receive God's grace and forgiveness as you say the first twelve verses of David's prayer of contrition together:

> *Have mercy on me, O God,*
> *according to your unfailing love;*
> *according to your great compassion*
> *blot out my transgressions.*
> *Wash away all my iniquity*
> *and cleanse me from my sin.*
> *For I know my transgressions,*
> *and my sin is always before me.*

*Against you, you only, have I sinned*
*and done what is evil in your sight,*
*so that you are proved right when you speak*
*and justified when you judge.*
*Surely I was sinful at birth,*
*sinful from the time my mother conceived me.*
*Surely you desire truth in the inner parts;*
*you teach me wisdom in the inmost place.*
*Cleanse me with hyssop, and I will be clean;*
*wash me, and I will be whiter than snow.*
*Let me hear joy and gladness;*
*let the bones you have crushed rejoice.*
*Hide your face from my sins*
*and blot out all my iniquity.*
*Create in me a pure heart, O God,*
*and renew a steadfast spirit within me.*
*Do not cast me from your presence*
*or take your Holy Spirit from me.*
*Restore to me the joy of your salvation*
*and grant me a willing spirit, to sustain me.*

PSALM 51:1–12

*We cannot escape the embarrassment of standing*
*stark naked before God. It is no use our trying to*
*cover up like Adam and Eve in the garden. Our attempts at*
*self-justification are as ineffectual as their fig-leaves.*
*We have to acknowledge our nakedness, see the divine*
*substitute wearing our filthy rags instead of us, and allow*
*him to clothe us with his own righteousness.*

JOHN R. W. STOTT

# Making It Real
## in Your Own Life

**1.** Set aside some quiet moments and read Psalm 103:8–14. Then write your own psalm of praise back to God, thanking him for the gift of his grace.

**2.** If you are still holding on to a particular "rock," ask yourself why. What will happen or be required of you if you let go? Maybe you owe someone an apology and haven't been willing to make amends. Perhaps pride or fear is getting in the way of the unburdening process. Consider loosening your grip just a little by making an "appointment with grace." Set a time to get together with a trusted friend, a priest or minister, a counselor, or any human being you have reason to believe will be compassionate and gracious as you share your struggle with dropping the rock. As much as you can, open your heart to this person's love and counsel. Sometimes the way to forgiveness is a long journey. Let a kind fellow traveler walk with you a while.

> *Learn to be patient with yourself. Enjoy the process of inner growth for what it is—an ongoing opportunity to become the best we can become at all levels of our life. Don't push the river. Just let it flow.*
>
> ELAINE ST. JAMES

# The Kiss of God

*R*edeem: *to get or buy back; recover; to restore to favor.*

That's what Jesus Christ has done for us. He bought us at the highest price ever paid in the history of time. We were lost, but now we're found. When we confess our sins to Jesus, he *will* forgive us and purify us (1 John 1:9). Through him we are restored to full rights of privileges as children of God.

A stanza from an old Welsh hymn sums up the awesome accomplishment of the cross:

> *On the Mount of Crucifixion*
> *Fountains opened deep and wide;*
> *Through the floodgates of God's mercy*
> *Flowed a vast and gracious tide.*
> *Grace and love, like mighty rivers,*
> *Poured incessant from above,*
> *And heaven's peace and perfect justice*
> *Kissed a guilty world in love.*

A holy God stooped down to brush his lips against the planet whose people had scorned him from day one. And over two thousand years later, sinners are still tingling with the thrill of his kiss.

No wonder the gospel is called Good News. When it has wooed us like a lover and overwhelmed us with grace, we are changed. Little by little it transforms our fear-bound, petty, bitter hearts into bold, compassionate, forgiving hearts that long to spread the News. When we have been kissed by God, we are compelled to kiss our fellow sinners with the passion of his grace.

> *When Paul caught sight of the love of God,*
> *he went off like a man possessed, running throughout*
> *the world, spreading the news at awful cost. When*
> *friendly hands tried to calm him down, when they*
> *urged him to take it easy, he shrugged them off*
> *and said "the love of Christ compels me."*
>
> JIM McGUIGGAN

# A Moment
# for Quiet Reflection

**1.** Reflect on everything you've studied and discussed over the past several weeks in regard to forgiveness. What one truth or insight has been most startling or helpful to you? Why?

**2.** Is there any belief about forgiveness you had at the beginning of this guide that you now believe is contrary to God's Word? If so, write it down.

# Knowing God's Heart

**1.** In the account of Jesus' horrific death is a snapshot view of the first human being ever saved by grace. Read Luke 23:32–43 together. We know virtually nothing about the crimes of the crooks crucified on either side of Jesus, but Matthew's account tells us they were thieves. According to verse 41, what was one thief's perspective on what was happening?

**2.** The other thief put in his two cents worth as well (verse 39). Discuss what you think he was thinking and feeling.

**3.** What does the enlightened thief's response to the hostile thief suggest about how we are to deal with those who are unrepentant for their sin and scorn?

**4.** Jesus' murderers placed a message above his head as he hung—helpless, they supposed—at their mercy (of which they had none). What was the purpose of the sign?

**5.** What does verse 42 imply about what the thief who spoke in verse 41 knew that most people on the scene didn't?

**6.** When the thief asked Jesus to "remember" him, what do you think he expected?

7. We are not told about the impact Jesus' response had on this broken man. What do you suppose went through his mind and heart as he awaited death?

8. If you were that thief and you had just been given the kiss of life in the face of death, what might your feelings be as you surveyed the hostile crowd? If you could come down off the cross, what would you want to say and do?

**9.** Even as his enemies pounded nails through his hands and feet, Jesus felt compassion for them. How can his short prayer in verse 34 help you when you are mistreated by others?

**10.** As we've learned, forgiveness does not require ignoring past hurt or pretending it doesn't *still* hurt. Rather, it involves canceling debt, extending grace, and acting out goodwill. Lewis Smedes says, "You will know that forgiveness has begun *when you recall those who hurt you and feel the power to wish them well.*" Discuss ways in which forgiveness has begun for you, if only a little.

> *God does forgive but it cost the breaking of His heart*
> *with grief in the death of Christ to enable Him to do so.*
> *The love of God means Calvary—nothing less!*
> OSWALD CHAMBERS

# Friendship Boosters

**1.** Biblical forgiveness is in some ways simple, in other ways incredibly complex. As God's lights in the world, we need help from each other as we try to follow Christ's example and shed his grace on those who need it most. Look back at the questions you wrote down in the "A Moment for Quiet Reflection" section of Lesson 4. If some of these questions are still niggling, write down one of them on a small slip of paper and drop it into a "hat" in the center of your circle.

**2.** One at a time, draw a paper from the hat and read the question aloud to the group. Then put your heads together to see if you can help each other come to some biblical conclusions. Since forgiveness is usually a process, commit to being each other's "sounding boards" in the future as you continue to work out biblical forgiveness in your relationships with God, yourself, and others.

# Just for Fun

Redemption is a joyful thing! Spend some time brainstorming about ways to express your joy and gratitude by doing "random acts of kindness" for others—be they friends or enemies. Designate one person to be the group scribe as you throw out ideas as fast as they come to you. Be creative, clever, magnanimous—and don't be afraid to be downright silly! From the master list choose one act of kindness you can perform for a woman in your group, and do it in the week ahead—anonymously if possible. Give the kiss of God in your own tiny way. Share the joy.

# Praying Together

Stand in a circle and join hands and hearts as you thank God individually for specific blessings and direction you have received as a result of your weeks of study and discussion. Close your prayer time by saying the prayer Jesus taught us aloud together:

*Our Father who art in heaven,*
*Hallowed be Thy name.*
*Thy kingdom come.*
*Thy will be done, on earth as it is in heaven.*
*Give us this day our daily bread.*
*And forgive us our debts,*
 *as we also have forgiven our debtors.*
*And do not lead us into temptation,*
 *but deliver us from evil.*
*For Thine is the kingdom, and the power,*
 *and the glory, forever.*
*Amen.*

MATTHEW 6:9–13 NASB

---

*Celebrate your relationships! Celebrate the lessons*
*from the past and the love and warmth that is there today.*
*Enjoy the beauty of others and their connection to you.*
*Celebrate all that is in your life. Celebrate all that is good.*
MELODY BEATTIE

# Making It Real
# in Your Own Life

**1.** Get out the piece of paper on which you wrote the personal belief about forgiveness that has become obsolete as a result of insight you have gained in the past several weeks. Dispose of the paper through some kind of ritual: burn it, shred it, flush it, bury it. In your own way leave the burden of your wrong beliefs at Jesus' feet.

**2.** On another piece of paper write down the name of one person you haven't yet completely forgiven. It might be someone long dead, or someone you still relate to every day (like yourself!). Lift the paper high over your head in a symbolic gesture of giving your resentment or confusion up to God, and ask him to give you clear insight and direction as you continue on the way to forgiveness. Write the date on the piece of paper and tuck it away in a journal, a drawer, or an old Bible. When you run across it in the future, you may have reason to praise God for the ways in which he's faithfully answered your prayers.

---

*One day I'll look back on all this and laugh.*

BARBARA JOHNSON

---

# LEADER'S GUIDE

## LESSON ONE

4. Joseph's brothers' terror when he first reveals his identity was probably due in part to the fact that he made his disclosure with no clear indication of how he felt about them. Was he furious with them? Did his tears suggest his ongoing anguish over what they'd done to him? Were they about to be condemned by this powerful man? In verse 4 Joseph does a couple of things that indicate he has forgiven his brothers. First, he asks them to "come close" to him. He is not speaking to them as a ruler to his subjects; he is willing to be personal and vulnerable. Second, once they are gathered round him he restates his disclosure in a more personal way: "I am *your brother* Joseph." By emphasizing his significant relationship to them he removes the barriers of time and position and takes the first step toward reestablishing his bond with them.

5. When we store up painful memories or hold onto resentment, we create a "time bomb" in our hearts: eventually the internal pressure will cause either an explosion of rage or an implosion resulting in soul-sickness. Joseph seemed to be experiencing the consequences of this twenty-year buildup of unresolved feelings, and when he finally had the opportunity to release them he could no longer control himself. What relief he must have felt as the truth tumbled out, grace flowed, and internal freedom came! Forgiveness has power to heal not only the offender but the victim as well.

6. It is crucial to note that even though many years had passed since Joseph last saw his brothers, he had in no way forgotten what they'd done to him. He identified himself as "the one you sold into Egypt." He did not sugarcoat that brutal fact. Even God, who says he "will remember [our sin] no more" (Jeremiah 31:34; Hebrews 10:17), does not literally forget our wrongs. Scripture is not telling us that we have an absentminded Father. Rather, his grace is so great that it swallows up all darkness so that God can look at us *as though* we had never sinned. Because of this aspect of his character, he chooses not to remember what he could rightfully punish us for. As we are filled more and more with the wonder of his grace, we too can "forget" others' sin in this symbolic way.

7. The fact that his brothers had wronged him was not the ultimate truth in Joseph's mind because he believed that God was completely in charge of his life. His faith in God's sovereignty and his acknowledgment that only God could judge the situation rightly enabled him to resist "blaming" his brothers. In Joseph's mind, the whole ordeal had been God's

will. (It is important to note that at this time Joseph had had over twenty years to process his experience and to watch how God brought good out of his suffering in many specific ways. It is probably unrealistic to expect us to have the kind of faith perspective Joseph had if we have only recently suffered harm. Forgiveness is a process.)

8. Joseph's story teaches us that we do not have to deny the facts in order to forgive. We can confront our offenders with the truth of what they did and let them see our pain. However, when we focus on God's character and plan we can look beyond the offense and the offender to how God can use our suffering for his good purposes. Through the eyes of faith we can view our offenders as guilty without needing to punish them. Joseph's brothers knew they deserved the worst of whatever he had to offer, and he knew it too; but because Joseph didn't rely on them for his well-being or continue to blame or credit them for the whole course of events, he was able to forgive them for their very real offense. He did not forget, overlook, or excuse their sin, but he did not make them suffer for their wrongs. Biblical forgiveness involves giving up our "right" to punish our offenders.

9. The weeping of Joseph and his brothers indicates vulnerability between them. They weren't keeping each other at "safe" arm's length; rather, they interacted with heartfelt emotion. The result was "talking," which implies intimate and easy fellowship rather than fearful posturing and hostility. The feelings of relief and joy in the text are almost palpable.

10. Joseph's brother Judah is no longer the hard-hearted boy who participated in victimizing Joseph. Not only is he willing to sacrifice his own freedom in order to assure his younger brother Benjamin's well-being, but he expresses great regard and concern for his father's feelings. In the past, none of the boys had cared a whit about the pain they would cause Jacob when they got rid of his favorite child. As soon as Judah passes this final "test" on behalf of his brothers, Joseph knows it is safe and prudent to reveal his secret. While Joseph shows his brothers extraordinary mercy, in no way does the text imply that it was extended entirely "free of charge." Joseph might have chosen to *forgive* his brothers regardless of their attitude and behavior (by letting go of whatever malice he had toward them), but he did not make himself vulnerable and *reconcile* with them until after he'd assessed their true character and judged them capable of relating to him with integrity.

12. Common misconceptions about forgiveness are indicated by statements such as

> "If I forgive, then I will have to pretend the offense never happened."
> "If I forgive, then I will have to be friends with the person who hurt me."
> "If I forgive, then I will have to open myself up for more harm."

"If I forgive, then I will have to stop feeling the pain, and I can't."

"If I forgive, then I will have to let my offender 'get away with it.'"

The story of Joseph and his brothers makes clear that none of these statements is true. Joseph didn't deny his brothers' cruel action or his own pain in response to it. He didn't hesitate to confront them with the truth, and the fact that he showered them with grace didn't mean he was excusing their behavior. Perhaps most important, he chose to have a new relationship with them only after testing their hearts and determining that their relationship could indeed be new. He did not open himself up to them naively or without regard for his own well-being.

*Friendship Boosters.* Have small slips of paper and pencils on hand.

# LESSON TWO

2.  Both of the older son's statements suggest a very sad state of affairs in his heart and in his relationship with the father who loved him. The first statement implies that the older son saw his father as an authority figure more than as a loving parent. Perhaps he felt like he had to "slave away" and please his father in order to be loved by him. It doesn't sound like his work on his father's estate was about serving in love or being in partnership as a member of the family; rather, it seems he felt obligated to his father, like a hired hand instead of a beloved son.

    The second statement is a bitter accusation against the one who didn't give him what he felt was his due. The rebellious younger son got to feast on his father's most choice livestock while the devoted older son didn't even get a cheap old goat, much less a party to celebrate his faithfulness. Again, the implication is that he didn't believe his father loved him, even though all his dad's possessions were his to enjoy. Because he didn't embrace and revel in his position as a son, he couldn't receive the love his father probably showed him every day.

3.  By referring to his brother as "this son of yours," the young man further distanced himself from the family. He wouldn't even recognize the prodigal as his brother, so intense was his hatred and bitterness.

4.  In verse 31 the father affirmed his love and devotion to his older son, as well as the young man's permanent position of value in the family. In verse 32 he tries to "close the gap" his son has created by referring to the prodigal as "this *brother* of yours." He goes on to appeal to whatever true righteousness might reside in his son's heart when he reminds him that in God's economy a sinner who repents is cause for rejoicing.

5.  Not only is God gracious and compassionate to sinners, but he longs for their return to him and is elated when they come home. He does not hold their sin against them, but continues to treat them as his beloved children no matter what they have done to hurt him. This tenderness

and graciousness extends to every flavor of sinner, including the self-righteous. Even in the face of his older son's rage and accusations, the father was gentle and appealed to the godly part of his son that he believed was there. God never gives up on us, no matter what our sin.

6. The prodigal approached his father with the utmost humility. He believed he had thrown away all claims to sonship because of his irresponsible and disrespectful behavior, and he had no thought of regaining his former position as beloved family member when he decided to seek shelter on his father's estate. He came to his dad broken, contrite, and empty-handed, and he owned up completely to his sin against his father and against God. He made no excuses for himself but threw himself entirely on the mercy of his father, hoping for nothing more than the status of a slave. Even though this parable emphasizes the lavish mercy of God, it teaches us that his love is not to be demanded as our due. God expects us to approach him in humble repentance.

7. When Jesus was on earth, his harshest condemnation was directed at the religious, upstanding citizens of his day. The older brother estranged himself from his father and brother through his pride, arrogance, and self-righteousness. He could have enjoyed rich fellowship with his family and experienced joy at his brother's return, but he thought he was "too good" for his own good.

10. These verses make it clear that each and every one of us is a sinner, no better and no worse than the next, and our denial of this basic fact is a grave affront to God. The older brother's self-righteousness estranged him from his father and brother. There is no place in the heart of the believer for hatred, so if we nurse our grudges and cling to our malice, even against those who "deserve" it, we must question the integrity of our walk with God. A disciple who wants to follow God wholeheartedly cannot afford to be "blinded" by the darkness in his heart.

12. Only God has the insight and wisdom to judge us or anyone else rightly. We need not take the burden upon ourselves to "balance the scales," and we can count on the fact that God himself will do so in his own time. If someone is "getting away with" evil, he will eventually stand before God where his intentions will be revealed. And if we are due praise and honor from our Father, we will surely receive it.

*Just for Fun.* Bring a blindfold.

## LESSON THREE

6. Obviously Jesus knew that human beings can't literally be perfect like God, so he must have had something else in mind. Matthew 5, 6, and 7 comprise a long sermon Jesus gave to his beloved disciples. In it he summarized a good deal of everything he had to say about how to live as his set-apart followers in the world. In order to stand out in society, includ-

ing the "religious" society of the priests and Pharisees of the day, Jesus' disciples needed to think and act very differently from the norm. Jesus was calling them to a high ideal, a whole new standard of philosophy and behavior that would surprise their culture. The "perfection" they were to strive for was intended to reflect this radical new covenant and call both pagan and religious hypocrite to an entirely different way of life.

8. When we come up with our own "paybacks," we tend to muddy up the scene and get in God's way. God states clearly, "I *will* repay." God is more concerned with justice than we are, and he will go far beyond "balancing the scales"; he will annihilate evil entirely, eternally. Only God has the wisdom to know what punishment really fits the crime; we can only guess based on what we can observe in our offender, which isn't enough on which to make a perfect judgment. In our ignorance we will be either too harsh or too lax, so it is crucial for us to trust that God knows what he's doing, even when people seem to get away with their transgressions. God despises evil and promises to avenge it; our job is to get out of the way and "leave room" for his wrath.

10. Treating our Christian brother or sister as "a pagan or a tax collector" is a way of breaking the sweet fellowship believers are meant to enjoy. This is part of Jesus' strategic battle plan against sin. He does not excuse or tolerate unrepentant offenders, and he doesn't ask us to either. We are to participate with him in the confrontation and restoration process. However, using the instruction in Matthew 18 to justify "punishing" our offenders with malice or "kicking them out of the group" just because we don't like something they did is abhorrent to God. When viewed in light of Jesus' complete teaching on sin, forgiveness, and restoration, we must understand this tough instruction as one more way to love our offenders back into fellowship. The whole intent of Jesus' teaching here is to win back our brother, not to permanently excommunicate him from relationship. Sometimes a "last resort" action in this winning-back process is called for: withholding the full rights and privileges of rich, intimate relationship until the offending believer's redeemed heart becomes so hungry for what has been lost that he or she returns to the "fold." When that happens, we are to extend a welcome. If a believer never repents for intentional wrongs he or she has committed against other believers and God, then that person's salvation may be in question. Jesus said, "'Not everyone who says to me, 'Lord, Lord,' will enter the kingdom of heaven, but only he who does the will of my Father who is in heaven. Many will say to me on that day, 'Lord, Lord, did we not prophesy in your name, and in your name drive out demons and perform many miracles?' Then I will tell them plainly, 'I never knew you. Away from me, you evildoers!'" (Matt. 7:21–23). We are to be discerning when dealing with sin in others, being careful to give them the "gift" most likely to bring them to repentance. As we'll see in the next lesson, sometimes

that gift is the "burning coals" of kindness; other times it is excommunication with a purpose.

11. Some of us mistake an "I'm sorry" for biblical repentance and foolishly set ourselves up to be hurt over and over by someone who is not genuinely intent on changing his or her destructive ways. The forgiveness Jesus is requiring of us here is the extension of grace to the one who is fully cognizant of the harm he or she has caused us, asks us for forgiveness, and sets his or her heart on change. Because none of us can have a perfect record when changing a negative behavior, sometimes we "re-offend" more than once on our way to complete transformation; thus the mandate to give a genuinely repentant offender multiple chances to prove the state of his or her heart. There is no instruction here, however, to put up with halfhearted efforts or to welcome mistreatment. The goal of forgiveness is always purposeful: to invite a repentant person to be restored to God and to us.

## LESSON FOUR

1. There is probably more than one answer to this question, but one suggested by Dr. Dan Allender makes a lot of sense. "What does evil expect?" he asks. "The answer is more of the same." The people who have harmed us with intent know, even if they are not sorry, that our natural response to them should be anything but kind. To meet an enemy's basic human needs (symbolized here by food and water) is to temporarily reverse the natural consequences of his actions and surprise him with undeserved kindness.

5. Christ did not have to die for sinners. He could have revealed his glory at any time by leaping down off the cross and overpowering his would-be murderers—and he was dared to do just that by those who ridiculed him (Matt. 27:39–42). By allowing his enemies to complete their murderous deed, he was preparing for the ultimate revelation: not even the grossest evil could conquer the love of God. His sacrifice and resurrection opened the door to forgiveness and salvation for any sinner who, in shame and repentance, accepts divine love so undeserved.

8. The implication is that it is easy to be overcome by evil if we just let it "roll over us" like a tidal wave. Evil is not to be tolerated; it is to be overcome. We are to fight evil and win! The only way to do this is to "know our enemy," face him or her squarely, and fight strategically. When properly understood as a divine strategic weapon designed to bring evil people to their knees, "doing good" can be the ultimate act of love.

9. Anyone who reads the gospel accounts of Jesus' life and death finds out that Jesus was no wimp. Myriad examples can be drawn from Scripture that show how Jesus knew exactly why he was here, what he was up against, and what it would take to accomplish his goal of vanquishing

evil once and for all. When Jesus interacted with sinners, he drew on his limitless creativity to wisely dish up a spiritual meal that would make both friends and enemies just sick enough to know they couldn't recover without his intervention. Jesus was anything but passive in his dealings with people; even his voluntary death was a powerful action designed to bring life to all of humanity.

## LESSON FIVE

4. The religious teachers and Pharisees set out to put Jesus in a no-win situation. No matter what his answer, they figured they could accuse him of being an insurrectionist. If he allowed the woman to be stoned, then he'd be in conflict with Roman law, which forbade it. If he said she shouldn't be killed, then he'd be considered a heretic who had no regard for the Jewish law, which required execution for some sexual sins. A natural response to being put in such a double bind would be fear, anger, capitulation. But Jesus appears calm and completely unruffled. Not only doesn't he argue with the religious folk, but he doesn't even seem to be paying them much attention. He's playing in the dirt, not even making eye contact as they pelt him with tricky queries. He doesn't join in with the moral dissection of the woman standing before him, nor does he appear to be horrified by what she's accused of doing. Throughout the Pharisees' diatribe Jesus remains composed and almost detached.

5. The religious guys' assumptions were wrong: Jesus could not be tricked, cajoled, or intimidated. He proved himself unpredictable yet again when he responded with a creative perspective on the problem they brought to his attention. He didn't "take sides" with either the law of the land or the Law of Moses. Instead, he introduced another slice of the new covenant by showing the hypocrites that there was an entirely different way to look at the issues. And it didn't put them in a good light! He turned their double bind around on them, leaving them speechless and impotent to harm the woman without condemning themselves.

6. When Jesus finally looked at the woman full in the face, she probably didn't know what to expect. Would he straighten her out now with a lecture? Would he give her a rigorous lesson in new covenant theology? She must have been surprised when he told her nothing but instead asked her to reflect on what had just happened. He wanted her to engage with him in a process of discovery. She was about to experience first-hand what his grace was all about.

7. The woman spoke only three words, perhaps with timid, awestruck wonder. Since Jesus had a reputation in town, she probably knew he was the sought-after rabbi everyone was talking about. She knew that adultery was a sin, that the Jewish laws against it were clear, and the punishment severe. Here she was, an exposed sinner, standing before a righteous man

who spoke for God. She could have launched into a passionate plea for understanding and grace. She could have made excuses for herself, demanded explanations, or hightailed it off the scene. Instead, she stayed put, considered Jesus' questions, and answered simply and respectfully, "No one, sir." We don't know for sure what was in her heart, but her quiet answer suggests a humble, hopeful spiritual posture.

8. Jesus' reassurance makes clear his mission on earth: he did not come to condemn repentant sinners, but to liberate them. He was not in the business of setting up a hierarchy of sin the way the Pharisees were. He'd just made it startlingly clear that all people, even the "religious," were sinners in need of grace and forgiveness. He gladly extended both to the sinner before him, setting her on a different path and releasing her to a new life.

12. It should be clear by now that God does not want us to live with the oppression of unresolved guilt. He offers us sweet fellowship with him and assures us that if we repent of our sin, we no longer need to carry a heavy burden. Because he has forgiven us, we are free to jump for joy and walk forward with confidence and dignity.

## LESSON SIX

2. One source of the second thief's hostility might have been his despair in the face of death. He knew he was getting his just deserts and that nothing could save him. When people have no hope, despair often displays itself in anger.

3. The wise thief rebuked the foolish one, reminding him of his sin and his need for mercy from God. We are not to simply "put up with" sin in others; rather we are to expose it and invite the sinner to repent. Sometimes this is done with direct confrontation, such as in verse 40. Other times our rebuke is delivered through the "burning coals" of kind action that has the power to bring evil to its knees.

4. When criminals were executed by the Roman state, their crimes were posted so all could see why they deserved death. Jesus was accused of claiming to be "the king of the Jews"—an assertion considered heretical because both Jews and Gentiles were expected to subject themselves to the rule of the Roman empire. Even in the minds of most Jews, Jesus' proclamations about himself were laughable because everything about him contradicted what the Jews expected their king to be like. He claimed to be their victorious ruler, yet he couldn't even save himself! Why should they trust him to save their nation? The sign hung over Jesus' head by the Romans was intended both to mock the Jewish hope for a Messiah (if this was he, then they were truly lost!) and to humiliate the Man who hung "helpless" and dying.

5. Most of the people in the crowd considered Jesus' claims of kingship to be ludicrous. Even most of Jesus' own followers who wept at his feet had lost faith in the fact that this dying man was their long-awaited Messiah. We don't know anything about the thief's religious training or personal background; we aren't told whether he'd ever heard Jesus preach or whether his faith was born in those short hours before death. All we know is that he recognizes some part of the reality of who Jesus is when he acknowledges that the dying Man will soon reign in his own kingdom.

6. We can only guess at how much the thief understood of the whole truth about Jesus' identity and authority. If he had not been following Jesus around and hearing his sermons, he probably didn't grasp much of what was promised to those who would be given the keys to the kingdom. It's possible that the thief's request for Jesus to "remember" him was not a fully enlightened request for eternal salvation, but rather a last grasp at hope that if only this holy Man would keep the memory of the thief close to his heart, perhaps the criminal wouldn't be entirely lost once his body became a lifeless shell. Theologian Frederick Buechner points out that to be "remembered" suggests that "even after I die, you can still see my face and hear my voice and speak to me in your heart. . . . If you forget me, part of who I am will be gone." Perhaps the most the dying transgressor was hoping for was to live on in someone's memory.

7. Again, we can only guess at what the thief understood about the implications of Jesus' words. But what a thrill it must have been to contemplate the possibility that even "today," the day of his death, he could hope for something more! Jesus assured him that when he ceased to breathe, he would not cease to exist, nor would he be alone.

8. We might assume that as more and more of the reality of who Jesus was dawned on the thief, he would want to "spread the news," to let the hostile soldiers and weeping disciples know that this Jesus would actually conquer death and that through him everyone could have "paradise." The New Testament is full of accounts of how the people who experienced God's grace were compelled to share it and warn the lost about the consequences of their spiritual blindness. If the thief had lived or been listened to as he hung dying, his wonder and joy would almost surely have spilled forth onto those who still needed enlightenment and salvation.

9. Even when we want to forgive, the dilemma is agonizing when nails are still being pounded through our hearts. The only way we can rise to such an unnatural task as forgiving those whose behavior or attitude continues to hurt us is by understanding that only a darkened, deceived heart is capable of inflicting harm with no remorse. If a relationship cannot be restored and enjoyed because of ongoing sin, sometimes the most we can do is acknowledge with grief that some people just "don't get it."

Before Christ's grace transformed our own hearts, we didn't get it either. Yet even in our darkened state, he loved us and extended grace to us in the hope that we would one day see the Light. We are to follow his example in our own relationships.

*Friendship Boosters.* Have small slips of paper, pencils, and a "hat" on hand.

*Just for Fun.* If possible, have available a large tablet on an easel, a chalkboard, or a white board so that everyone can see the list as it is being compiled.

# FAITH

Women of Faith Bible studies are based on the popular
Women of Faith conferences.

Women of Faith is partnering with Zondervan Publishing House,
Integrity Music, *Today's Christian Woman* magazine, and Campus Crusade
to offer conferences, publications, worship music, and inspirational gifts
that support and encourage today's Christian women.

Since their beginning in January of 1996, the Women of Faith conferences
have enjoyed an enthusiastic welcome by women across the country.

Call 1-888-49-FAITH for the many conference locations and dates available.

www.women-of-faith.com

**See the following page for additional information
about Women of Faith products.**

**Look for these faith-building resources from Women of Faith:**

*Friends Through Thick & Thin* by Gloria Gaither, Peggy Benson,
Sue Buchanan, and Joy Mackenzie
   Hardcover 0-310-21726-1

*We Brake for Joy!* by Patsy Clairmont, Barbara Johnson, Marilyn Meberg,
Luci Swindoll, Sheila Walsh, and Thelma Wells
   Hardcover 0-310-22042-4

*Bring Back the Joy* by Sheila Walsh
   Hardcover 0-310-22023-8
   Audio Pages 0-310-22222-2

*The Joyful Journey* by Patsy Clairmont, Barbara Johnson,
Marilyn Meberg, and Luci Swindoll
   Softcover 0-310-22155-2
   Audio Pages 0-310-21454-8

*Joy Breaks* by Patsy Clairmont, Barbara Johnson,
Marilyn Meberg, and Luci Swindoll
   Hardcover 0-310-21345-2

*Women of Faith Journal*
   Journal 0-310-97634-0

*Promises of Joy for Women of Faith*
   Gift Book 0-310-97389-9

*Words of Wisdom for a Woman of Faith*
   Gift Book 0-310-97390-2

*Prayers for a Woman of Faith*
   Gift Book 0-310-97336-8

We want to hear from you. Please send your comments about this book
to us in care of the address below. Thank you.

## ZondervanPublishingHouse
*Grand Rapids, Michigan 49530*
http://www.zondervan.com